# 100 WAYS TO Love YOUR WIFE

## MATT JACOBSON

SPIRE

© 2019 by Faithful Families Ministries, LLC

Published by Revell
a division of Baker Publishing Group
PO Box 6287, Grand Rapids, MI 49516-6287
www.revellbooks.com

Spire edition published 2023
ISBN 978-0-8007-4258-4

Previously published in 2014 by Loyal Publishing

Printed in the United States of America

Unless otherwise indicated, Scripture quotations are from the King James Version of the Bible.

Scripture quotations labeled NKJV are from the New King James Version®. Copyright © 1982 by Thomas Nelson. Used by permission. All rights reserved.

Baker Publishing Group publications use paper produced from sustainable forestry practices and post-consumer waste whenever possible.

23   24   25   26   27   28   29      7   6   5   4   3   2   1

For my sons, that in striking blows
in favor of civilization,
you might know and never forget
how to love as Christ loves.

# 100 Ways to Love Your Wife

This is a book of ideas—ideas that, if followed, will lead you toward an excellent marriage.

An excellent marriage sounds good, doesn't it? It also sounds like an endangered species. Epic marriages are pretty rare these days.

But they don't have to be—not for you and me.

The best, richest marriages are enjoyed by couples of every age group who know a simple yet all too often forgotten truth. Great marriages are the result of husbands and wives making a lot of everyday choices that say "I love you" rather than "I love me."

If you want an epic marriage worthy of the best love poet, country-western singer, playwright, novelist, or the Song of Solomon, then learn how to say "I love you" through all the normal days of marriage you are given.

That's the challenge, isn't it? All those days. They need to be filled with something, but most of us run out of ideas to keep marriage fresh. This book provides those ideas.

Not long into my marriage, I discovered that just because I was satisfied and happy didn't mean Lisa was. I needed to learn and understand what every smart husband knows: continually filling your wife's reservoir is an ongoing endeavor, but doing so pays amazing dividends.

A loved woman—a cherished wife—is a giver, returning to her husband far more than he ever poured into her soul.

But it doesn't happen all at once. If you take the simple steps outlined here and are consistent over time, you will enjoy a transformed marriage—a marriage transformed by love.

Life is short. Love her well.

They shall be one flesh. (Gen. 2:24)

He who loves his wife loves himself. (Eph. 5:28 NKJV)

# Introduction

I'll never forget those eyes dancing above the rim of her glass the moment I walked into the room—the first dance of many . . . wild and wonderful.

As I lay across the bed from my beautiful, lovely bride during our Hawaiian honeymoon (a typically generous gift from my brother and sister-in-law), those dancing eyes held my gaze, their radiance intensifying a vague sense of loss.

Time. Suddenly all those years without her seemed lost.

As I drank in the moment's wonder, my fingers fell high on her cheek, lightly tracing to her lips the soft outline of her face.

"Why didn't I meet you ten years ago? Where were you? Look how much time we've missed being together."

But life is like that, isn't it? One day we wake up in an oasis, wondering why we wandered around in the desert for so long.

I purposed right then and there, twenty-one years ago, lying on the bed in our room on the fifth floor of the Lahaina Shores Hotel on Maui that I would cherish this woman, my bride, this breathtaking gift from God, every day of my life.

How great it would be to report that I have loved Lisa perfectly. I cannot. I've caused her tears, been unloving, insensitive, and downright sinful at times. But I can report to you that Lisa has been and is a cherished woman. I'll be transparent . . . she makes it easy for me.

I reach out from the inside to let her know how much she matters to me. She knows that it's serious business with me. Lisa is my priority because Jesus Christ made her my priority—and He expects to be obeyed. He wants me to love her as He loves His Bride.

Jesus is the example for every Christian man to know how to truly cherish his wife.

*Wait a minute, Jesus isn't married!*

But He is (or soon will be). His Bride is the Church.

And Christian men are instructed to love their wives as Jesus loves His (see Eph. 5:25).

You see, if you claim to be a Christian man, being the husband of a cherished woman just isn't optional. It is the call of God on your life—to preach the gospel with the power of your love for your wife—an expression to the world of how Jesus Christ loves His Bride, the Church. If I don't cherish Lisa, I'm walking in sin and I must change. The same is true of every married Christian man—he is sinning if he is not cherishing his wife.

Scripture says that when you love your wife, you are actually loving yourself. Because according to God, the two of you are one single entity. And a truly cherished wife takes great pleasure in returning that love with interest.

What do you have to lose?

She gave her
heart to you.
# VALUE IT for the
## *sacred treasure* it is.

Every wife has a deep desire to be cherished—to be of su-
preme importance and value to her husband. If your wife's
friends were asked the question about you—Does he cherish
his wife?—how would they respond? Is the answer obvious
to them? What would your wife say? Does she feel cherished?
To truly value her is to leave no doubt in anyone's mind, especially hers. Remind yourself often that you've been entrusted
with something beautiful, something sacred. Then communicate to her that you know it and that it matters to you.

# REACH
## for her
### *often.*

Has it been more than one day since she felt your arms around her? As husbands, we get our needs met and then allow too much time to pass before we show affection through physical touch . . . meeting her needs. She loves to feel your arms around her, often. Do you have the kind of job that takes you away for extended periods of time? If so, then regular physical touch when you are present is even more crucial.

# After a busy week, run a **hot** bath ... just for her.

Occasionally, slip unnoticed into your bathroom in the evening, run a hot bath with bath salts, light candles, turn on soothing music (whatever you know she will especially enjoy), and then tell her something is waiting for her in the master bath. Leave and lock the door behind you, making sure nothing will distract her for an hour as she spends the whole time thinking about how fantastic you are!

# Ask about her thoughts *and* dreams.

Initiating a conversation that has your woman as its focus tells her heart that she matters to you, that you see her as an important person with her own ideas and dreams. In this way, she's no different from you. You want to be affirmed by being sought out as a person. So does she.

*Listen*
**when she answers,**
not because you have to
but because the person you
*cherish*
is sharing her
**HEART**.

Listening with interest says "I truly value and respect you." What you hear are her words. What she hears in your understanding, engaged interest is a reassuring voice that says "I love you."

# *Romance* her
before, during, and after
## the wedding . . .
### e s p e c i a l l y
**after** the wedding, **after** the
honeymoon, **after** the kids start
to come, and **after** they begin
to head off to college.

So many wives wish their men would romance them—to do something that says "I'm thinking about you and want you to know how much I love you." Sex may go a long way in saying "love" to you, but it's only a small part of what says "love" to her. Don't stop loving her in nonsexual ways just because life got busy. Even when you're old together, she will never grow tired of being romanced by you.

# Buy her the *best chocolate* you can afford and keep her stash well stocked!

At any given time, there might be approximately four married women on the planet who don't like chocolate. For the rest of you who have chocolate-loving wives:

Step 1—Find out what kind of chocolate your wife likes. Light, dark, truffles . . . get specific intelligence. It's important!

Step 2—Leave chocolates on her pillow, on the dresser, conspicuously in the laundry room, in her closet where she's sure to find them, on her desk at work. It's not really about the chocolate; it's about saying "I've been thinking about how to delight you, about how to make you smile."

# Shower together every chance you get.

Trust me, you just should.

# Tell her you *really appreciate* the dinner she made or that baking effort every time.

Love makes the simplest meal a feast. But if we're unwise with our words, we can turn a gourmet dinner into a famine of the soul. It's her heart on that table in front of you. Remember, you care how she feels. You cherish her heart. Don't diminish her with a careless or snide remark, or with no remark at all. With the right perspective and a wise, loving approach, you can give even burnt casserole its merits.

When she goes into that kitchen, she is making another attempt to say "I love you." If something turns out a total disaster, you can always and honestly say, "I'm sorry it didn't turn out the way you had hoped, but I appreciate so much the love that inspired you in the first place and I can live on that kind of love forever."

# Kiss every day,
## but more importantly,
### kiss with *passion*—
### every time you kiss.

A simple kiss on the cheek can be a throwaway gesture or an experience that contains the whole Book of Love.

# Send her away ...
## because you *love* her!

She needs to relax and recharge, so from time to time, send her somewhere away from the busy world you both inhabit.

She'll have so much more to give if you look after her needs in this way.

# Hold her close,
## until she feels the
# STRENGTH
## of your conviction.

Your wife has a heightened sense of the care you have for her. For the most part, she doesn't want a hug that says "You're my pal." Husbands can communicate much with a hug, so don't give hugs that say "Whatever." She wants something more. Give the kind of hugs that say "I love you, a lot!" When you hold her, make sure she knows where your true feelings lie. Make her a believer in the depth of your love with hands and arms that leave no room for questions.

# She's confusing you again, isn't she?

Some women are better at communicating than others, but the fact is that occasionally our wives send conflicting messages—conflicting to us, at least! To them it all makes perfect sense. When this happens, it's time to listen to Billy Joel's song "She's Always a Woman" and remind yourself that she isn't a math equation—she's more like an Impressionist painting. Then smile and tell yourself how much you love her.

# You've removed your clothes, but have you removed the OBSTACLES?

She wants to be sexy with you, so help her be free and un-inhibited by being the guardian of her privacy, her dignity, and her honor.

# *Surprise her* with a spontaneous mini-date.

Coffee, smoothies, herbal tea, kombucha. Know what she likes, take her to that little hole-in-the-wall café she loves, add conversation about the day, and suddenly you're having a date with your girl and she's feeling loved.

Wait a minute. You just spontaneously decided to go out for no particular reason and have a drink together . . . just because you like being with her?

You're making all her friends jealous, but that's okay. Keep up being a good example for all the other husbands. They might take a hint. Marriages need a lot more husbands like you!

# Express *thanks* for the thankless jobs.

When was the last time you vacuumed, folded towels, or mopped the floor? Some guys may respond, "Oh yeah, that's me!" but for most, not so much. Notice and openly tell her how grateful you are that the laundry is done and the clothes are folded . . . again . . . and again . . . and again . . . (if you haven't been grateful, get grateful!).

Who doesn't appreciate their work being noticed? And it's all the more meaningful when *you* notice it. She works hard—with much on her mind—managing, nurturing, and loving, for most of which she rarely hears a thank-you. When she feels your appreciation, she feels loved and valued, and her spirit soars.

# Let her know you see her
# STRENGTHS
### and unique gifts,
### and tell her you value
### them.

Your wife is a smart woman (she married you, after all, right?!). She could run a country. Build her up with positive words. "You were amazing when you . . ." "You are really good at . . ." "I'm really impressed with your ability to . . ." It's as simple as offering praise openly, often, and sincerely.

# Make her your accountability partner.

What could be easier than telling your guy friends all the ways you've failed when there's no possibility of rejection and they've fallen in all the same ways you have? Real accountability is about "not going there"—not about the fellowship of failure.

Allow no shadows in your relationship. Live honestly and tell her everything. There may be some pain at first, but if you are humble and broken, it will make you stronger. If you've committed to face your wife with honesty and openness, suddenly being accountable has meaning and the path of shame and destruction doesn't look so good anymore.

# Tell her often,
## *"You are so beautiful."*

Because she is,
   and she needs to hear you say it
   . . . because she forgets.

# Take her on a "h o u s e k e e p i n g   d a t e ," but don't tell her.

Arrange for a housekeeper to come and clean your house while you and your bride are enjoying a dinner out. You could hire a service or just involve some friends and family to come in and clean. Do you have older children? Ours are often in on the plan. What wife doesn't like coming home to a clean house, especially after a dinner out?

# When it comes to *making love*, gently ask her what she likes.

Then follow through, with the goal of delighting her. Don't be defensive if she mentions something you're doing that she would like you to change. Remember, it's about delighting her.

# When it comes to *making love*, gently help her understand what you like.

But make sure she doesn't sense from you that she's getting it wrong. Never, ever be critical or condemning. This is sensitive territory, so any suggestion that you disapprove or aren't pleased with her will be an instant turnoff. She wants to please you. Keep it positive.

# When it comes to making *love*, hold nothing back.

Give all of yourself—heart and soul, along with your body. Remember what the Good Book says: the two of you are "one flesh" (Gen. 2:24).

**When you find your dream girl, life is great.**

Lisa and I started out having coffee together every day at the espresso place down the street from our apartment. We only needed one chair. Or should I say, one chair and one lap. Trust me, it was *very* comfortable.

A few decades down the road and we're still at it—coffee together every morning.

I'm an early riser, which is perfect because I love making coffee for my woman (and now my older daughters too). It's routine—the same every morning: grind the beans, put into the two French presses just the right amount, skim the cream from the raw milk, get the bowl of raw sugar, find Lisa's porcelain cup with the little birds on it, and warm up my cup with hot water before I pour in the coffee. Then I put it all on a tray and serve it to Lisa on our back porch (summer) or in the living room, near the fire (winter). I love serving her coffee, just the way she likes it.

Once in a while, when our roles are reversed, the same thing happens. She warms up my cup with boiling water because that's the way I like it . . . because she loves to serve me.

What if I didn't know she always prefers the porcelain cup with the little birds on it?

How could she know I want my cup warmed up before the coffee is poured in?

These things aren't "right" or "wrong." They're just preferences—what we like.

A loving relationship is made up of delighting to serve your spouse—and so is lovemaking.

Wouldn't it be great to understand what your spouse prefers? What she doesn't like and what she finds appealing and relaxing? What she finds arousing and what turns her on? Couples don't know because they don't seek each other out. Because they don't ask. Because they don't talk.

This isn't hypothetical. Lisa and I have had this conversation. We're both glad we did, and so is God. When it comes to intimacy, He wrote the book.

**Here are five things you can do to get the conversation going:**

1. *Timing is important.* Make sure you talk when your spouse can give you their full attention (no distractions and away from the kids).
2. *Choose a place.* Pick a place where your spouse will be comfortable openly discussing the details of your intimacy.
3. *Make it special.* This conversation is special, so make the moment special. What does your spouse like? A quiet walk while holding hands or dinner at a favorite restaurant or sitting close on the couch?
4. *Start the discussion focused on her needs.* The needs and desires of your spouse should always come first. It's always easier to listen *after* you've been heard.
5. *Know what you're going to say.* Begin by saying something like this: "I've been thinking about our lovemaking and I care a lot about delighting your heart, about pleasing you. Am I meeting your needs? How about your desires? What do I do that you like? Is there anything you'd like me to do that I'm not doing or could do differently?"

When it comes to your turn to talk about what you need and like, be sure to start by being grateful for the things your spouse does that you like and appreciate—keep it positive.

Remember, romantic lovemaking is God's idea. He created you and your wife to delight in each other. It's easy to forget that the Song of Solomon is in the Bible. You should read it sometime.

# Speak with
## *gentleness.*

You can make her hard and tough, but she didn't start out that way. She's a woman. She needs to be cared for. Care for her with the tone you use. Harshness will close her spirit toward you. Gentleness will open her spirit.

Pleasant words are as a honeycomb, sweet to the soul, and health to the bones. (Prov. 16:24)

# ACCEPT that she thinks *differently* from you.

A wise husband doesn't want a "rubber stamp" wife who automatically validates everything he thinks and wants to do. She sees things differently and that is a very important benefit of her personality. Value it. Don't minimize her unique perspective and intuition—it's a God-given gift to help you make wiser decisions.

# During moments
## of frustration,
# NEVER FORGET:
### what God has put together,
## let no man tear apart.

There's no getting around it—some moments in marriage are filled with frustration. When those moments come, never forget that God chose her for you and, even in the midst of frustration, you have some things to learn: things like controlling your temper, not giving full vent to your anger, learning to listen, not responding in kind, and more.

> A soft answer turneth away wrath: but grievous words stir up anger. (Prov. 15:1)

# Seek her counsel.

Many wives say their husbands don't care about their opinion. Don't be that guy. It's not only foolish but also wrong. The two of you are a single entity, so don't run off and act on the latest idea you and your buddies talked yourselves into. Be prudent. Seek her counsel.

# Listen to her *wisdom* after you've sought her counsel.

So you asked for her counsel, but did you truly listen? Many wives say their husbands never listen to them. Such a man is a fool. Instead, avail yourself of the wisdom and perspective God blessed you with in your wife.

# When she returns from the salon,
## it's time for you to start talking.

Compliment her on her new haircut or hair color or hairstyle or manicure or whatever it is that she has had done. Even though you've been married for a while, she's never stopped enjoying that you notice her. It's just another way of telling her, "You're my girl!" And that *never* gets old.

# As a woman,
### she's always pouring out,
## so remember that
## it's your job to *always*
## pour in.

No woman remains fulfilled on great moments from the past. "Relationship" is always present tense. "Pouring in" simply means doing those things that make her feel loved and cherished.

# NOTICE
### that new outfit—
## she's dressing for you.

Don't let her arrive home in a new outfit from the store without telling her how great she looks. If it's still in the shopping bag, just say, "Hey, would you like to model that for me?" and persist, even if she's shy about it. And one more thing. Remember that in these moments, she's not looking for your analysis or opinion, unless it's along the lines of "You look amazing!"

# Keep your relationship *frisky* from the honeymoon to year sixty and beyond!

It's more fun that way, and no matter how many years have passed, she still wants to be the object of your desire. There's not a single reason to let her pass you in the hall without giving her a playful _____ (you fill in the blank). And besides, when the kids become teenagers, embarrassing them by being affectionate with your wife in the middle of the kitchen is a whole lot of fun too!

# *The* little engine that **could** needs a little rest.

Make sure your wife gets the regular rest she needs. She may keep chugging along like the locomotive in *The Little Engine That Could*, but you know that without rest, she's going to crash. The fact is, there are few priorities that can't wait until she's gotten proper rest. When it comes to her fatigue, be the Enforcer. She'll appreciate you for giving her "permission" to rest and for creating the circumstances to make it happen. Besides, when her needs for rest are met, she has more energy for all sorts of fun things!

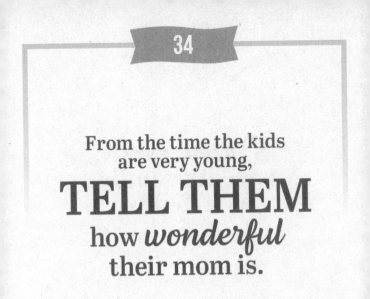

From the time the kids
are very young,

# TELL THEM

how *wonderful*
their mom is.

For wives and mothers, appreciation from the kids is like
protein to muscles—it fills her with strength to meet the
endless demands of her calling. And you're meeting your
responsibility by reinforcing what God wants them to do.

Honor thy father and *thy mother*. (Exod. 20:12, emphasis
added)

# *Praise her* to parents, family, and friends.

Look for opportunities to let everyone know how deeply you respect your wife and how proud of her you are. At some point, your thirdhand compliments will get back to her—and they will delight her heart.

# NEVER
make negative comments
or inferences or give
disapproving vibes
## about your wife
to anyone.

Don't make the huge mistake of speaking negatively of your
wife to others, and especially to extended family. As soon
as everyone understands that the two of you are one single,
unassailable entity, they'll learn to respect her and she'll love
you for it. Trust me—it makes for a secure woman, and a
secure woman is a happy wife.

# NEVER
## put up with even
### slightly critical
## comments about your
## wife from anyone.

Don't let the moment pass. Whenever someone says something critical about her, turn directly to the person and say, "I don't appreciate that kind of comment about my wife." Never leave any doubt about where your loyalties lie.

# Admire her
## with your eyes.

When you were dating and/or soon after your wedding, you were really good at this. There's no reason to stop now. In fact, now you have a lot more reasons!

# *Admire her*
## with your words.

Don't let a day (that's right, not even one day) go by without speaking a positive, adoring word to her. If you're not present, use an email or a text, or a quick phone call. Even the simplest words of admiration (if sincere) will run deep—all the way to her heart.

# Banish
## s a r c a s m
# from your
## speech.

Sarcasm might be funny on a sitcom, but in a real marriage, it's a paper cut that won't heal. Leave the sarcastic comments that damage women and tear down marriages to other, lesser men. While those guys are scratching their heads wondering why their wives don't want to have anything to do with them, you'll be building something beautiful on a solid foundation.

# Plan a
## stay-at-home
# date.

If you have kids, make plans for them elsewhere. Get some takeout food, a few candles, and give her a long, slow back rub. Did you know that a gentle back rub is braille for "I love you" and all sorts of other intimate messages?

# *Embrace* the reality that the two of you make up *one* distinct entity.

Family and friends are on the outside looking in. Be wise and seek counsel, but don't allow others to unduly influence you and pry into your private lives before you're ready to share. You don't owe them personal information. And if they're offended? Don't worry, they'll eventually get over it. As for the few who don't, too bad for them. No one (including family) belongs on the inside of your relationship until you've invited them to be there.

# You were made
# STRONG
## for a reason,
## so act like a man
## and shoulder your
# responsibilities.

Husbands, likewise, dwell with them with understanding, giving honor to the wife, as to the weaker vessel, and as being heirs together of the grace of life, that your prayers may not be hindered. (1 Pet. 3:7 NKJV)

# Take the lead.

When it comes to dancing, only one can lead. There's one CEO of Apple and there's only one president of the United States. Marriage is no different. Apathy is like dry rot to a marriage. You're in the position of husband, so do what good husbands do: lead with gentleness and collaboration, but lead.

# NEVER
## contradict
## your wife in public.

We've all been to a party with the couple who thinks their personal argument should command the attention of everyone in the room. Decide you're not going to be that couple and save disagreements for private conversation—away from everyone, especially the kids.

# It's *movie night* at home, but forget *Rambo.*

Occasionally, surprise her and pick a chick flick you know she will enjoy and then shock her socks off—enjoy it with her! So chick flicks aren't your thing? Watching one once in a while won't kill you and you might really enjoy the way the story ends. WARNING: If you can't completely do this with a whole heart—if you're unable to prevent sighs, huffs, yawns, and disparaging remarks—you might want to take a pass on this one!

# Your *anniversary* matters, even if she says it isn't important.

Just do yourself a favor and decide right now that you are going to make a big deal about your anniversary. You don't have to do anything expensive or extravagant. Setting aside a day or even a few hours to celebrate (or two nights away if you can swing it) is simply the smart husband's way of communicating value, love, and care. No man ever regretted cherishing his wife by celebrating their anniversary.

# Write a *love note* and leave it on her pillow to find later.

I can sense the resistance from here. So, you're not a poet? No one is suggesting you become one. But come on! There are only about a million variations on "Baby, you're the *best*!" And the simple act of buying a generic card (the kind I always get) and writing a few sincere words that capture what you think of your awesome woman will make her feel like one in a million.

# Hold hands.

When you go for a walk, a drive . . . actually, hold hands
everywhere you go. Holding her hand is an easy way to whis-
per "I like being connected with you."

# Keep your *heart* at home, even when you travel.

Teach yourself that the *best* place is at home, by her side. You are not a victim. You make the choice when faced with the many inducements to pull your heart away from what is best and highest.

No man ever made a snap decision to be unfaithful. When men allow their hearts to be pulled away from the home, it's a long, incremental process, so recognize your responsibility to keep your heart desiring home.

A man with roving affections has an insecure wife who is always begrudging his time away with the guys. A man whose wife knows his heart is at home will practically kick him out the door to spend time with his buddies.

# *Pray* for her.

God has invited you to pray about all things. Are you praying for what He has identified as one of your most important priorities?

# Ask her to *pray* for you often.

As a man, you typically have far more needs and concerns than you may acknowledge, yet your best prayer partner—the one who knows you from the inside—is right beside you. Mention something specific that you would like your wife to pray for you this week and make it a habit. Caring for each other in this way draws you closer together.

# Your wife's radiance
— her countenance —
## in large measure
is a *reflection* of how well
she is loved by you.

If, in your case, this is good news, then congratulations! If it's bad news, then do yourself a favor. Take responsibility and get busy adding a sparkle to her eyes by what you do and say.

# You don't own
# your body.

Your body, including all the parts, doesn't belong to you. It belongs to your wife, so it doesn't get to go places and do things she doesn't know about and wouldn't approve of (see 1 Cor. 7:4).

# Let her satisfy your *passion*.

The only people who think God is a bit of a prude who frowns on sex haven't bothered to get the facts—some of them fairly steamy. Here's how the Bible puts it:

> Let your fountain be blessed,
> And rejoice with the wife of your youth . . .
> Let her breasts satisfy you at all times;
> And always be enraptured with her love. (Prov.
> 5:18, 19 NKJV)

Sometimes husbands can overlook the fact that for wives, physical intimacy involves a sacred giving. When something sacred is given, we should express our deep gratitude.

# Choose contentment *with* her.

Remind yourself often that you are content with this great gift God has given you. The world will scream the opposite message to you, so you've got to counteract that false voice with the Voice of Truth. Listen to only that voice and you'll build something with the strength to go the distance.

# Surprise her
# with a picnic and a
# stroll afterward—
## and take care of all the details.

If you're like most men, this is just the kind of thing you're not great at. But, seriously, how difficult can it be? A couple of sandwiches, fruit, drinks, a blanket, and napkins, and you're good to go. With just a little effort, you're in the running for the "Most Romantic Day with My Woman" award!

You've shown
*appreciation*
and that's good.
# EVEN BETTER
to help with the work
around the home.

It's vital to express gratefulness for all she does, but there's more. Yes, you work eight-plus hours a day, five days a week, but she (especially as a young mom and/or working mother) works 24/7, so don't expect her to do it all.

# Helping with the vacuuming isn't a **substitute for** *romance* (for most women).

You are willing to help with the chores. That makes you one of the "good ones," but never let yourself believe working around the house is a substitute for romance. It might be a welcomed gesture, but helping with housework and picking up the living room aren't necessarily stand-ins for "taking her away from it all."

Marrying Lisa, I knew I'd hit it big. We were on our way to "epic" marriage status about four months into it. All that was necessary was *Super Husband*, and he was there, so we were good to go!

So why was Lisa in the kitchen with *that look* on her face?

*That look* . . . the one that says "I'm not happy and *you* are the reason."

It was time to put my foot down, which always makes conversations between husbands and wives more interesting. Please forgive us, ladies. Sometimes we just can't resist, even if the result is more like stepping on something in the barnyard than clearing up the problem.

But was that going to stop me? Uh . . . no.

"Okay, so what's bugging you?" I asked in, well, maybe not the most loving, gentle way. Which is kind of natural when you know you are the answer to the question.

She didn't answer—at least with her mouth.

The flames (the ones coming out of her eyes) and her hands did the talking as she vigorously dried a dinner plate and set it down with that decisive air you use just short of it shattering into a thousand pieces.

Instead of breaking the plate, she shattered the silence.

"You take me for granted."

"Take you for granted? Are you kidding me?! I'm practically Superman around here. I don't know one other guy who does the stuff I do *all the time*! I help with the dishes, I help fold the clothes, I fixed the washing machine myself, I vacuum, I . . ."

Facts are sooo helpful in moments like these. Talk about ungrateful.

It's a good thing towels don't break. She threw it on the counter and turned to face me. "I don't care if you do *any* of those things. I just want you to take me out for coffee more than once in a blue moon. But most of all, I just want you to want to be with me."

"But I am with you. All the time! That plate that just survived a near-death experience? I was standing next to you washing it two minutes ago, remember?"

"That doesn't count."

"Doesn't count? Are you telling me that all my work around here to prove I care and love you counts for nothing?"

"I didn't say 'nothing,' but, well, helping with the housework is next to nothing compared to how I feel when you want to spend time with me, away from all the stuff that has to be done."

Wow, who knew love was so easy? Just communicate that you want to be with her, that you want her, that you want to be close. Time away with her from the demands of the day communicates love to her. It's not rocket science.

Sometimes we're so busy communicating to our wives in ways that say "love" to us, we miss that she might be different. What says love to you may not say love to her.

And the best part is that it's easy to find out what says love to her. Maybe for you it's talking over a cup of coffee in some funky little shop she loves. Or just go ahead and ask, "Hey, gorgeous, if you had to name three things that make you feel loved by me, what would they be?"

# Tell her
## you *need her*.

Occasionally, whispering "I need you" with sincerity meets a deep need in her soul. She wants to—no, she *needs* to—feel needed by you physically, yes, but also as a person who is helping you become a better man.

# Tell her
### w h e n
## you *need her.*

Be bold and tell her the truth. The fact is, you *need* her physically. Most guys don't want to admit they need anything because they feel instinctively that doing so communicates weakness. But it doesn't, not to your woman. She wants to satisfy your sexual needs and desires. And you do need her. Sex is something you were designed to need. And that's a very good thing. God made you this way.

# NEVER, ever look (interestedly, longingly, lustfully) at another woman with your eyes—or indulge lustful thoughts.

Train yourself to turn your eyes away at every opportunity that presents itself. And don't tell yourself this convenient lie: "I just can't help it." You *can* help it! Your flesh just doesn't want to.

Don't lie to yourself. If you're scouting, you're hurting your marriage by dishonoring your wife. Stay in command of your flesh and honor the woman God gave you . . . and honor the God who gave her to you. Be faithful in this area.

Every act is preceded by a thought. This is why foolish men become unfaithful. They told themselves no harm was being done. After all, they were only *thinking* about it. It wasn't like they were actually going to *do* it.

True faithfulness—the kind that will keep you out of trouble and is approved by God—is total faithfulness. After all, the two of you are one. That includes your mind.

I will set no wicked thing before mine eyes. (Ps. 101:3)

King David ignored his own advice and paid a heavy price, but you don't have to. The Bible says, "There is no temptation you face but that which is common to every man; but, God is faithful, who will not allow you to be tempted beyond what you are able to face, and will, with the temptation also provide a way of escape so you can endure it" (1 Cor. 10:13, author paraphrase).

God has provided the power for you to triumph in the face of temptation. Exercise that power, escape the temptation, and honor your wife.

# Get away *together*.

If at all possible (our true priorities are almost always possible), purpose to get away together for a couple of nights at least once a year.

# Speak words of truth, delivered with *gentleness, love*, and *support*.

A lot of guys feel they can never say anything evaluative or corrective to their wives. In many cases, that's because they ignore the context, the timing, and the spirit in which it is done. Remember that old adage "People don't care how much you know until they know how much you care"? It's especially true of our wives. Cultivate caring before you ever correct. Give careful attention to these matters before you purpose to speak. If I have something of a corrective nature to say, I ask God to help me say it in a manner Lisa can hear and to give her the grace to hear it as it's meant.

# Be loyal.

Always take her part. She needs to know, down to her socks, that she can always count on you to have her back. Never be evaluative of her to a third party. When it comes to marriage, be a partisan, not an adjudicator. Save the evaluation for private conversation between the two of you. In public, always present a solid, united front.

# Show *approval* by the way you look at her.

She can *feel* what you're thinking and what you're feeling—whether or not you approve of her, of what she said, or of what she is doing. Your countenance and general demeanor are important because her expert, no-fail radar is always scanning, picking up your signals.

# Recognize she's the weaker vessel and don't complain about it.

From time to time, life is going to be overwhelming—that's just the way it is. Don't expect your wife to keep soldiering on with that fourth dinner party in a row, that next group of out-of-town guests, and the fifteenth activity that week while keeping everything else running. For the sake of order and sanity, sometimes you'll just have to say no or deal with these demands alone. She can do a lot, but she can't keep doing everything. Loving her means being understanding, protective, and reasonable with her limits.

# Make Valentine's Day irrelevant with expressions of your *love* all year long.

Yes, you should do something for Valentine's Day (even if she's the type who says it's not important to her), but one day a year for love? Seriously? Men who truly love their wives just can't wait 364 days before expressing their love again.

# Tell her you'll be
## *faithful forever.*

We live in a fallen world—something she knows all too well. Forget the general public, how about your average gathering of Christians? Divorce is more common than the cold virus. She knows you're a good man, but it's encouraging and reassuring for her to hear, occasionally, that your commitment to your vow before God is as fresh in your mind as the day you uttered it.

That's why I wear the *FAITHFUL MAN* wristband. It's a strong statement of who I aspire to be and my commitment to my wife. Lisa loves that every woman can see a public statement of my faithfulness to her.

If you're interested in checking them out, go to Faithful Man.com/shop.

# Act and speak
# with *kindness.*

A kind husband is a safe husband. She needs your kindness—and it's the right thing to do.

> Be ye kind one to another, tenderhearted, forgiving one another, even as God for Christ's sake hath forgiven you. (Eph. 4:32)

# There is no shame
in your "oneness"—
be naked *together*.

God is in favor of nakedness. The story He wrote starts out with two naked people in a garden! And He called it very good! He gave you each other to enjoy. Because He made the two of you one single entity, there is no shame in being naked together, in private. Enjoy each other's nakedness. Enjoy each other's bodies. Consider the Song of Solomon. Remove the euphemistic references to fruit and you've got a solid R rating—and it was all God's idea. Take the opportunity to enjoy what He has given to you. But remember, men, if you want your wife to enjoy being naked with you in private when the lights are low, love being with her in broad daylight.

# Speak with *grace*,
### e v e n   ( e s p e c i a l l y ! )
## when she's not
## showing *grace* to you.

When she's not at her best, respond to her with the kind of grace you wish to receive when you're having "a day." The husband who offers grace when it is least deserved also gives grace when it is least expected, most needed, and will do the most good. And by doing so, you're doing exactly what God has done for you.

# *Forgive* with a whole heart.

Some forgive and never mention "it" again. And that's good, unless they continue to harbor anger or bitterness over the incident. When you truly forgive, you let it go, move on, and enter back into full fellowship. The only other option is a root of bitterness that will eventually grow into something ugly and destructive. Let it go and refuse to take it back.

# NEVER
## mention today what was
## *forgiven* yesterday.

Even in the best marriages, disagreements come and, for most, arguments happen. But there's a place you should never go when dealing with a difficulty in your relationship. If you've granted forgiveness for something, never speak of it again. It's that simple. Oh, you'll be tempted to bring up the past, but don't do it. When we yield to our emotions and bring up something we've already forgiven, we prevent our relationship from progressing forward. Remember: forgiven means forbidden.

# When you disagree, stick to the issue.

When the offense is brought up, it's typical to respond with the thirty-seven things she did wrong. This is just pride getting in the way of addressing an offense. Don't try to defend yourself by bringing up a single thing she did. Just listen to the offense and respond (in the Spirit) to it. If you don't, you'll quickly discover it wasn't worth "winning" the argument with your list of "facts." Pride makes a mess of everything it touches, and what's worse is that it puts you in opposition to God.

God resisteth the proud, and giveth grace to the humble. (1 Pet. 5:5)

# Choose *unity*— cling to each other in hard times.

Hard times will come. That's just what life does—it dishes up the hard stuff from time to time. So decide the following before you enter the valley: *nothing is going to come between us—nothing!* And remember, you play how you practice, so choose unity before it gets difficult and you'll cling to each other in the storm.

# Your responsibility
### and **authority** come from
## *God*, not **from your**
## personal power,
## s o l e a d  h u m b l y.

You're going to give an account of your words and deeds
and how you led. Never forget that you are accountable to
God—in everything.

# BE EXCLUSIVE
### and don't keep part of yourself in reserve.

Let her know she is the only one who is 100 percent on the inside with you. There's a great sense of security and strength that comes from knowing you're facing life with your soul mate. Many wives feel they are alone because their husbands rarely talk to them about what's happening in their world, including what they're thinking or feeling. This is not a personality trait. It is a choice . . . a wrong choice. You may be the silent type. That's fine for the rest of your relationships but not for your marriage. Open up, communicate, and make sure she knows you are walking through this life together with her.

# You're the *conductor* on this train.

Where are you going? Communicate your vision for what you want your marriage to represent—for who the family is becoming under your leadership. Your "people" need a vision—who you are and what you are about. What is the vision you are casting for your marriage and family? And because you married (or are going to marry) an excellent woman, she'll have some excellent input.

# Choose to be *happy.*

We all choose our perspectives on those things God has called us to walk through. Sometimes husbands forget the massive impact they have on their families through their general attitude. What kind of spirit are you bringing to your marriage and home? No joy in life? This has far more to do with you than with your circumstances or with other people. It's much easier to be joyful if you focus on how much you've received . . . how much you've been blessed. When you choose to be positive, you'll lift the spirits of everyone around you—especially your wife.

# *Love your wife* by taking precautions to protect yourself.

With random offers of internet filth in your inbox, there are countless ways to be unfaithful without even leaving your house. Counterfeits will always present themselves, so let your wife know they are nothing compared to the real thing: her. Recognize these counterfeits for what they are— enticements to destroy everything of value that you've built. Put safeguards up and establish for yourself God's standard: a zero-tolerance policy. You'll not only maintain your self-respect but also have a secure, happy wife and, best of all, the approval of God.

# Don't take the bait.
## Let go of
# harsh words.

It's inevitable—put two sinners (even really nice ones like you and your lady) in a relationship and you will eventually find a reason to disagree, strongly, and to argue, which occasionally may escalate into some harsh words. And it's made all the worse because you know you are 100 percent correct and she is dead wrong! And then there are all those ridiculous, outlandish accusations: "You're not . . ." "You never . . ." "You always . . ."

How does it make you feel when her words characterize you as some thoughtless, insensitive barnyard animal? Not exactly the stuff of heart-to-heart fellowship and oneness before God. At some point, and to some degree, this will happen, and what will you do then? Will you allow your mind to seethe and foam because of those harsh words? Or will you choose not to take offense, understanding that when her blood is up, she's capable of saying things that in her heart of hearts she doesn't believe are remotely true?

When we choose to walk in the flesh and become heated, we're capable of hurtful words. Don't take them to heart. They're not true, and she doesn't even believe them, which she will say when you both ask forgiveness and make up. Let those words go and they won't have a hold on you.

# Be a *generous giver* of second chances.

Nothing is more natural to the flesh than to stand in judgment of another person when they have committed a genuine mistake or wrong. *You don't deserve to be forgiven,* we hear our minds say as we feel the consequences of someone else's actions. But haven't you needed grace for the mistakes or bad decisions you've made or the hurtful actions you've done in the past? I'm pretty sure you don't get what you deserve, and neither do I. Be quick to offer the grace you desire when you find you've made a mistake. Truth is, you have been given second, third, fourth . . . many chances. Don't stand in judgment of your wife. Be quick to extend grace.

> If you won't forgive men of their sins against you, your Father (God) will not forgive you. (Matt. 6:15, author paraphrase)

# Whatever you plant *grows*, so what are you planting?

A woman never slams the door of her heart all at once. The age-old adage is "You reap what you sow." This is especially true in your relationship with your wife. And we're *always planting something*. The weeds grow easily. Fruitful plants take careful planting and regular care, but when we're attentive, what a great harvest! Sow wisely with your words and deeds.

# You were made to *initiate*.

She was made to respond, so make sure every day that when it comes to your loving her, she never runs out of things to respond to.

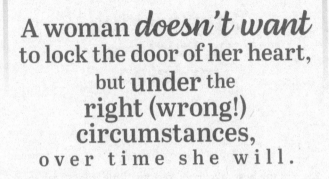

A woman *doesn't want* to lock the door of her heart, but **under** the right (wrong!) circumstances, over time she will.

Each time you neglect her needs, the door to her heart will close incrementally, bit by bit. And once it's closed, short of a miracle of God . . . forget about it, her heart is gone forever. So be wise and recognize what you do to encourage the door of her heart to open ever wider and to diminish the impulse to close it incrementally over time.

# Stop making
## the little things
# important.

Even in the best marriages, various "little things" can crop up in any given day—annoying little things, frustrating little things. So it's not that such things are absent from great marriages. The only difference is, the couple enjoying the great marriage has chosen not to dwell on them. We've got to remember something very important about these little things: they just don't matter. If we focus on them, they take on a destructiveness completely out of balance with their true importance. In every great marriage, there are big things to address. A wise husband saves his attention for those and lets the rest go.

# Schedule your weekly *date night.*

Wow, that sounds boring, doesn't it? But for most, it's necessary. If you rely on spontaneity for the time you spend with your wife, she often finds herself competing against urgent priorities—a competition that never makes her feel good and that she often loses. Happy wives know they are a priority for their husbands. Scheduling a date night may sound incredibly boring, but it doesn't have to be. If you schedule that commitment (and respect that schedule), you make a statement that nothing is more important than your time with her—a message she loves to receive.

# Don't expect *your wife* to make the arrangements for dinner out.

Asking your wife to handle the details of date night once in a blue moon is fine, but don't let it become a habit. She wants you to take the initiative for these things—just like you did when you were dating, remember? It's another way to show where she ranks on your list of priorities.

# Come up behind her and *kiss* her on the back of the neck.

There are very good reasons for this, but I bet you already know them!

# RESIST
### the impulse to try to change her.

Changing someone isn't your job, and the effort always results in hurt feelings and often much worse. Furthermore, there are probably things about you that she feels need to change as well. If there is something you truly would like to see changed, take your concern to God and leave it there. Changing people is His specialty.

# Remember your
## *wife's birthday.*

Put this date on the calendar and defend it against all competing priorities. Doing something special on this day, even if it is a small but sincere gesture, is important. Everyone wants to be remembered—even the wives who say, "It's not important." Answer this self-deprecating statement with "Oh, yes you are!" by celebrating and honoring her on this special once-a-year day.

# Go on a
# cheap date.

Pick up some ice cream from the drive-through (or coffee or whatever she would like) and then keep driving. Tell her all the mundane details about your day and ask about hers. A "driving date" might be cheap, but the message that you want to be with her is of immense value.

# Don't
## overreact
## to her mistakes.

Chances are (okay, guaranteed!) you've made a mistake or two, no? Allow that your wife may make a mistake from time to time. Give her the grace you allow yourself (and want from others) when you make a mistake. She already feels badly about the consequences. No need to pile on. Did she have a fender bender, an overdraft, a _____ (you fill in the blank)? Love her with compassion, sympathy, and a non-condemning spirit, and help her deal with the situation.

# EVERY TIME
### you walk in the door, look into her eyes and greet her with a *smile*.

That first connection at the end of a busy day is so important. In an instant, with a loving look, you can establish the tone for the evening that follows. A simple, purposeful, intentional gaze in her direction when you greet each other says "I've been waiting to see you all day, and I'm so glad to be with you!"

These are thoughts that warm the heart of any wife, thoughts that your wife desires you to have and to express, thoughts that are so easily communicated with a simple, loving gaze when you walk through the door.

# Tell her
# your schedule
# in advance.

Don't just expect her to flex her day around errands and plans you spring on her at the last minute. Letting her know your schedule ahead of time is simply the thoughtful thing to do.

# Ask her if there is something you can do that would say *"love"* to her.

Plan for this conversation. Take her to a quiet place where she can open up, and ask the question with genuine sincerity. The question itself says so much about your desire to care for her, but the follow-through on her answer will draw you even closer together.

# Love your wife by drawing near to *God*.

Ask God to do the necessary surgery in your life to remove those things that are not honoring to Him and to your wife. Ask Him to change you to be the husband He intended when He brought you and your wife together. If you are sincere, He will do it.

> Draw near to God and He will draw near to you. (James 4:8 NKJV)

# Keep the
## biblical standard
## and ideal in front of you
## at all times.

There is much in the Bible that will transform the marriages of men from almost any background and any religion—even someone who subscribes to no religion. But for the Christian man, the core requirement is clearly stated in the Word of God—and it's not optional.

> Husbands, love your wives, even as Christ also loved the church, and gave himself for it. (Eph. 5:25)

This is a problem because, the truth is, this standard for Christian marriage is, humanly speaking, ridiculous. You can't measure up to loving your wife as Christ loves the Church and gave Himself for her, and neither can I.

Fortunately for men (and women!), there is more to the story. Galatians 2:20 says, "I am crucified with Christ: nevertheless I live; yet not I, but Christ liveth in me." When the life of Christ animates what husbands do, a lot of wives are loved as Christ loves the Church and what was ridiculous becomes reality in your marriage and mine.

Yes, it's a high standard. Would we expect Jesus to establish anything less? He expects nothing less from us.

# Make a decision to *love.*

Choose to love. Always choose love. Every day, this choice presents itself many times and in many ways. If you choose to make decisions that say "I love you" rather than "I love me," then you are on your way to a great marriage.

And one last thought. A great marriage isn't today's destination; it's a lifelong journey of two spouses learning to love richly through all the seasons of their life together. Why not get started today?

**Matt Jacobson** is the founder of FaithfulMan.com, an online ministry encouraging readers to love God and walk faithfully according to the Word. Matt is a biblical marriage coach and mentor and is co-host (with his wife, Lisa) of *FAITHFUL LIFE*, a weekly podcast focusing on what it means to be a biblical Christian in marriage, parenting, the local church, and culture.

Matt attended Multnomah University in Oregon and studied philosophy at Trinity Western University in British Columbia. For twenty-five years, Matt has been an executive in the publishing industry. For the past sixteen years, he has been pastor and elder of Tumalo Bible Fellowship, a thriving community of Christians with a purposeful discipleship focus on biblical marriage, family, and church leadership development. He is a marriage coach and the author of the bestselling book *100 Words of Affirmation Your Wife Needs to Hear*. For more information, visit FaithfulMan.com/coach.

# Simple, Loving Words to Encourage Your Child
## EVERY DAY

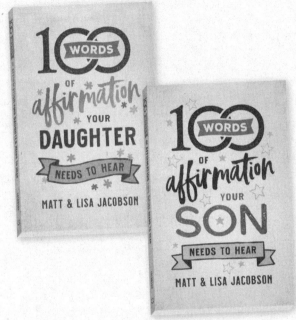

Matt and Lisa Jacobson want you to discover the powerful ways you can build up your child in love. These books offer you one hundred things to say that will help your son or daughter feel empowered, inspired, and deeply loved.

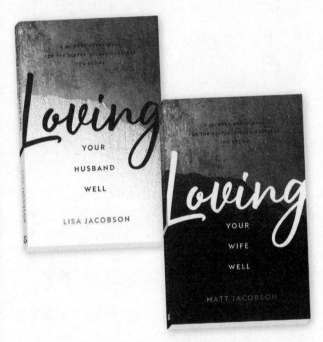

# Connect with
# MATT and FAITHFUL MAN!

# FaithfulMan.com

Cohost of the *FAITHFUL LIFE* Podcast

@FaithfulMan